I0212783

Works of the Heart

Works of the Heart

By LL Walker

Walker Publications®

Published by Walker Publications®
www.walkerpublications.co

Works of the Heart by L.L. Walker

ISBN **9780988250833**
Book ID
Poetry, Spirituality, Coming of Age

Acknowledgements

Life brings special people into our path for purpose and possibilities. This has always been my experience, even at times when I may not have fully appreciated them at the moment our paths intersected... but without them, there would not have been passionate moments to share with you.

To those who have brought those moments onto my path, to those who have encouraged me to come out from behind the curtain and share those moments... and to those who will read each page and say, "that reminds me of a time in my life when....." this book is for you.   *LL Walker*

Works of the Heart:

Poetry & Passages

Love is alive and demonstrated in so many daily things we do. If we are unaware we could miss these moments of two beings loving one another.

Writing poetry passages began when I was in the 6th grade. My teacher would have us memorize long poems of beautiful words, flowing and lingering in our minds as we mastered each stanza.

In this set of works, I have intertwined various love moments, mother & son, father & daughter, first loves, new loves, eternal loves...and love experiences we revisit that rekindle the inner smile of our soul.

A short Author's Note to give you a little insight into the story behind the writing is included at the end of many of the poetry passages.

Let's spend a little quiet time together sharing some of those warm moments of love and life.....in "Works of the Heart".

In Love...LL

Contents

Poetry:

Contents

Contents

Passages:

The You of Me--
Mother and Son

Our relationship is hard to explain,

Especially to those outside.

I am no longer my own person.

I am constantly aware of you.

I go about my daily routine—

Always conscious of you,

We share secrets.

You move—I smile—Nobody Knows.

I can feel your thoughts without your speaking.

I can sense your reaction to the surroundings.

We share everything from food to frustration.

We inhabit the same physical space.

You have made my sensitivity raise.

You have made me feel special.

Your life depends on me,

And soon mine will depend on you.

Once this phase is over,

This oneness we share,

Your life will just be beginning,

And I will still be there.

Author's Note:

The look of dismay staring back at me in the visor mirror of my car...fifty-five minutes ago I was an individual, free agent, soon to be college graduate. The reflection I see looks the same, but my awareness has been changed forever and I sit searching for a visible difference that wasn't there.

The day before, my doctor's office called. My blood tests were back and I was to stop by his office on my way to campus. Several of my friends had mono and I had all the symptoms—nausea and exhaustion. I had been accepted into graduate school as a teaching assistant and had no time to be ill.

Much to my excitement, "No mono," the doctor reported. As I got up to leave he said, "Please have a seat, we did find the origination of your symptoms." I must have looked panicked because he quickly added; "You are expecting a baby sometime in early August."

Pre-natal vitamins in hand, I headed to my car in a fog of disbelief. In the privacy of my vehicle I was searching for visual proof, but found none. I wrote this poem during a Sociology class a few months into this shared body experience.

A beautiful healthy boy became part of my life plan my first semester of graduate school.

LL Walker

Forgiveness —

Father & Daughter

The sun peaked into my room thru the tiny space between the curtains. I lay there quietly listening to my dad breathing his "still asleep" breath in the next room. I could hear mother in the kitchen on the phone with grandma.

Time alone with my dad was so special, and this was my chance. Quietly on tiptoes, I crept into the room he shared with my mom. I loved looking into his face. He had dark, almost black hair, a small scar above

20

his left eyebrow, soft cheeks, and the biggest hands of anyone I knew.

Closer and closer I leaned into his sleeping face. Suddenly...the covers flew back and those large hands grabbed me, lifted me up onto the bed next to the handsomest man in the whole world.... my world.

Tickling me, he laughed and in his deep voice asked, "What are you doing in here so early?"

"Nothing", I giggled as he moved to arrange the pillows behind his back and sat up. I knew he was sitting up so I could get into my special place nestled under his arm with my ear on his heart listening to it beat. His big hand reached for mine as he began stroking my fingers.

"Where's mom?" he asked quietly.

"*Downstairs talking to grandma on the phone.*" *I explained.*

"*Would you like to go to grandma's today or maybe to the park?*" *he asked as he coughed just a little.*

"*Uh-huh*", *was all I could say peacefully content.*

When my dad was around everything was safe and fun. I knew he loved me, not by his words—although he told me plenty—but by how he looked at me.

Today was so special because he was home. We just sat there quietly for a while then we heard mother coming up the stairs.

"*Quick,*" *he said,* "*let's hide.*" *So we pulled the covers over our heads trying really hard not to giggle.*

"Now where could Susan and daddy be?" she whispered pretending not so see those 2 bumps at the top of the bed.

"Here we are mommy," I squealed as I popped out from under the covers.

"Well, good morning," she laughed. "What are the two of you plotting for today?"

"Thought we'd head down to the park for a while and then maybe run up to mothers," dad answered reaching for a cigarette.

That was my queue to wiggle out from the covers and get dressed. "Hold on Lula Belle, where are you off to?" dad asked looking around mother who was checking his temperature.

23

"*Daddy, I'm not Lula Belle, I'm Susan.*"

"*Oh, pardon me...where are you off to Miss Susan?*" *he smiled.*

"*Getting my clothes so we can go to the park,*" *I explained excitedly.*

"*Hold on, I need to check your dad's bandages first, then breakfast, then dressed,*" *mother explained.*

"*Ohhkaaay*", *I replied, frowning and sulking as I exited the room, not liking it one bit that she was slowing me down from my "Big Plans" for the day.*

"*Hey, little Missy,*" *dad called after me,* "*this will only take a few minutes. Pick out a book and we can* read while mom gets breakfast on the table."

With renewed energy I called back a thrilled, "OK! I'll pick out a good one."

"You spoil her", I heard mom scolding him. "I know and I plan to do so her whole life", dad replied.

But this giant of a man wouldn't spoil me my whole life. A few months later, he left me for Jesus. I don't think he wanted to go without me, but everyone said I was too little and couldn't go.

You see my dad went to a place called Korea. I never really knew where it was, but he said it had mountains, pretty flowers, and bad men.

He went with his friends who all belonged to a club called, "The Army". Dad's job in the club was to jump out of airplanes and catch the bad men to stop them from hurting people...and little girls just like me.

One time as he was jumping out of the airplane the bad guys hurt him, so he had to go to a hospital and get better. Then, another time, he helped his friends 'cause the bad men were hurting them.

As he was helping his friends, the bad men hurt him again, but this time the club sent him home to grandmas to get better.

That's when he met my mom, got married, and had me. But, after a little while, whatever the bad men did to him in this Korea place kept making him sick and the doctors couldn't fix it. I heard my mom and grandma talking about pieces of metal in his body that moved around making him bleed on the inside.

Then one day, he went to a hospital and Jesus came to get him to take him to heaven. I love Jesus and I love my dad, so I guess if he couldn't be with me.... it's really a good thing he could live with Jesus.

Grandma says one day, I will see him again when I go to live with Jesus, but I wish daddy could have stayed with me just a little longer.

Maybe the hardest thing is to forgive the bad men that hurt my dad. I wonder if the bad men knew that when they hurt my dad, they hurt me too.

Grandma says forgiveness is very important and it makes Jesus happy when we forgive people who do bad things to us.

So, I will try, but right now I just miss holding my dad's big hand and seeing his love for me shine in his face.

Author's Note:

The first man a little girl falls in love with is often her father. Fathers have a special role in the life of their little girls. Our first experiences of loving a man and of a man making us feel special, loved, and safe are with our fathers. They become the measure by which we compare all men throughout our lives.

Psychologists tell us we pick men who remind us of our fathers. In my experience and those of my close friends, I would say that our relationship with our fathers plays a huge role in our partner selection.

I remember those feelings as a little girl. When my father died, I built a wall around those loving memories to protect myself from ever going through a hurt of that magnitude again.

My grandmothers and his siblings (my aunt and uncles) provided a connectedness to him for me. I love them for sharing him with me, but my best times have always been alone in the quiet where I can feel him close by.

My dad was the third son, fourth child in a family of six children. He was handsome, athletic, funny, loving, kind, and yet a man's man. The guy you stopped by to pick up if there was going to be a fight and the one who drew high school girls to their windows... as he walked home after basketball practice.

At seventeen when most boys in town were making graduation plans, he enlisted in the army, as had his brother before him. Jobs were scarce and the army meant he could send money home to my grandmother.

At Fort Benning Georgia, he became a Paratrooper. These soldiers parachute behind enemy lines and fight their way back to the front, catching enemy soldiers in-between. He was promoted to Sargent his first year.

The more he jumped, the more money he made, and the more he could send home to my grandmother. Three occurrences of physical wounds in battle ended his time in theatre. A bronze star, Purple Heart, inoperable shrapnel, and the respect of so many he served are what he brought home.

Working on my family genealogy was a natural evolution to add the details to stories I had compiled about my dad all my life.

As I expanded my search, I got to know this mountain of a man from people who knew him as a boy, a dreamboat, and a hero. Stories of practical jokes, breaking bricks with the side of his hands, and the intense pain he endured from the shrapnel in his body.

Maybe he knew he wouldn't be with me long or maybe he did, as my uncle use to say, "He thought he was the only man who could sire a child once you were born," his role as my father was his top priority.

He went to "Daddy School", took me everywhere he went, and held me at every opportunity. I wrote this passage after placing new flags on his grave.

The Fork in the Road

Preparing for another life move to

another city. Sorting and packing to lighten the load...when quite by accident, I ended up back to high school today. I found a box of high school essays, papers, and poems.

I also found a person with the same ideals, hopes, dreams, and desires as the person I look at today in the mirror.

I have come to many forks in the road over the years. Lived in many places, traveled to even more. Have experienced great success, joy, love, along with moments of deep sorrow and dismay...but today I learned in the heart of my heart, I am essentially the same.

I Wonder

I wonder about love.

I wonder about life.

I wonder how both can be.

I wonder if love will enter my life, or not even bother with me.

I wonder if my future will be like my past, or be something new and free.

I wonder if friends are all they seem, or if they are all just a dream.

But the one thing I wonder about most in my life is why the Creator made me.

Author's Note:

A large crab apple tree was one of my favorite places to read and write when I was in the 6th grade...that time in our lives when we aren't really feeling like kids anymore, but are too young to be teenagers.

You have your first menstrual cycle; your body seems to be moving faster than the rest of your emotions. Boys seem more interesting in a different way at times, but not all the time.

My favorite story was Cinderella...prince, a carriage, a great dress, and a beautiful heroine. What a life! I wrote this poem sitting in my grandmother's crab apple tree on a sunny summer day pondering my Cinderella life ahead.

The End --or

The Beginning

Even though we are apart

And I'm no longer first in your heart.

I want us to be good friends.

For that's the way true love should end.

But maybe in the fall,

We'll find our love's not dead at all,

Just hidden very deep inside,

Or covered up by foolish pride

40

But if this is our love's true end,

I want you to remember always

"You've got a friend".

Author's Note:

You are certain it will last forever. The first boy, who captures your heart, makes you his steady girl and transforms you into a couple.

It all seems so perfect. He moves into your mind, emotions, and schedule. Your every waking moment is about him. Time passes and you begin to plan your life together after high school. It's the logical next step...right?

Well not always. My first love experience was one of those perfect scenarios, until it wasn't. The nemesis of many a first love is distance.

We were sure that his leaving for college would not change our long-term plans or change the love we were experiencing. After all, doesn't absence make the heart grow fonder?

The first few months he came home every weekend, then we decided (actually he decided and I wanted to look mature, so I agreed) to still love each other but date other people. That sounded as crazy then as it does now writing those words.

Distance over time had put us on different life paths with a gap that couldn't be closed once I arrive at college. I missed the "us" of my best friend that love euphoria, and me. I wrote this poem as he was leaving for his second year at college and I was starting my final year of high school.

A Sense of You

It's the warmth I feel, just knowing you're around.

Reading books I know your eyes have read;

Your mind assessed;

Listening to music you listen to;

Humming in harmony to the memory of your voice;

Knowing we look into the same sky;

Are on the same Internet.

The smile I can't suppress, just knowing you're around.

44

The lightness of step, which can't be helped;

A private giggle of secret thoughts of you;

Idle daydreaming of what you could be doing;

Visiting restaurants we've shared and will again;

The peace of loving and being loved;

The anticipation of your next idea;

The excitement life continually offers, just knowing you're around.

Author's Note

Shiny and new right off the college campus I was launched into months of non-stop first experiences~ business lunches, airplane trips to Chicago for two-hour meetings, interviewing perspective employees, my first secretary and office...and of course my first office romance.

We worked for the fastest growing computer company of that decade. Long hours of work and travel wrapped in a bow of adrenalin rushes. I was sent to Dallas to help with the sales recruiting in the district there when we first met.

How to buy a cowboy hat, custom boots, and the Texas two-step were things he taught this small town girl form the Midwest. Distance didn't exist between calls, emails, and joint business trips; we spent what free time we had together.

The times apart are remembered in the poem, "A Sense of You". Young and career driven, when he asked me to marry him I declined.

He continued to be a good friend teaching me about business, acting as a sounding board as I made career moves, and making sure I knew he would be there if I ever needed an old friend to lean on.

LL Walker

Two Become One

Passion.... can you ever explode from holding passion too tightly or for too long within your own being? What is the purpose of passion, the energy it creates, and the urgency it generates? You are here with me, but I *can't touch you physically. I can touch your heart, your mind, your dreams; you're knowing of the possibility of me, but not yet the physical you.*

To hear the tone of your voice, each syllable flows from within you. The anticipation of this makes my desire blaze magnify to an almost unbearable level within, but lusciously wonderful.

A time for release, speed of ecstasy, needing to release my energy into yours; to feel the two of us vibrating into orgasmic experiences what can only happen to those united as we are united.

Knowing without speaking, seeking to calm our desire as we mark the time for our unification together.... physically together to enable the merging of our spirits in the same place, the fire enlarges who we are, blesses those around us, gathers to us those who we have come forth to heal.

My breathing is quick and fast; short rapid breathes as you move ever closer to me. You lay your hand on my breast feeling my heart. The delay is increasing my heart rate, my energy, my passion; my awareness emerges from the unknown into the known slowly to allow our intensity to grow at the pace it was agreed. Enabling us to rise to higher and higher places we know are there, but have yet to experience for our souls and ourselves.

You softly say, "Come let me hold you in my arms quietly as you return to me here in the physical, co-existing here and there, creating a thread of movement between our two worlds which takes us to higher unity with love, with Spirit, with one another, and those we are here to show the way."

Slowing my breathing, I respond, "Your hands are soothing across my back and shoulders, stroking my hair, holding my face between your hands peering deeply into my being; with you I am fully integrated. My love for creation moves to places of enlarged capacity I have never known."

We lay under a tree peering through the branches up into the sky as dusk settles onto the earth. We are one with each other and with mother Earth. We are one with the Spirit and our soul families. We are one and each of us is enraptured by the growth and light we bring into one another becoming a beacon of light, of hope, for those who feel despair.

Your arms around me unite our hearts into rhythmic beats in unison, harmony, and the pure energy of love. Now that you are here, our work can begin together. Feeling you, seeing you, smelling you, holding you...abundance of being, blessings, and love.

Author's Note:

Wedding days are filled with traditions, optimism, future plans, and eager innocent love. Months of planning are now memories. The anticipation of the bride builds in preparation for her entrance. The nervous groom does one final check of his cummerbund and tie. Both breathing abnormal patterns as their life together "till death do them part" begins.

The visuals missed in the wedding pictures are the rushing thoughts and emotions captured in this passage. Back and forth between what is happening and their daydreams of what will happen as this lifelong journey together begins.

He touches her to calm her at the altar. She remembers the picnic in the park when he proposed... so many thoughts and actions blending together as they become one.

Was this your experience on your wedding day?? It seemed to have been so on mine.

LL Walker

Anxious to see your smile....

The morning sun illuminating ever so slowly the sky as night's darkness disappears into the light announcing the beauty of the beginning of the day.... this is my heart's response when I see you smile.

You are generally a serious, thinking person filled with kindness and a sense of responsibility toward all who know you and even many you do not.

While there are those who smile continually encouraging others to smile in return; those passing in stores or walking along the street; your smiles are different. They are special. They are not rare, but also *not plentiful making them all the more important when they occur.*

Some would classify many of your smiles as a grin at best and I would agree. Regardless of the name, they are still very special and worth the wait to see.

At times your smiles are motivated by intellectual humor, or questions only a small child can ask. It's as though your smiles are so special that your heart holds them in reserve to only be released at those particular moments when there is a happening or event no other response is will do.

There are however those moments, when you think no one is watching you. Those moments when you are watching me read a book, or bathing the dog, or planting a flower that I see you smile.

A gentle, peaceful captivating smile, that can't be withheld, because it is at those moments, I know your heart is so full of love, your heart releases a smile to ease the pressure a heart filled with love created in the soul of a man as he admires his woman.

It is during those moments when you think no one is watching that makes my heart leap with the joy of your love and the light of your smile.

Author's Note:

Less is more was a nice phrase that never had much meaning until I met a man who made less seem like so much more...a quiet observant demeanor, long dark hair and a full beard to match. At times it was like looking into the face of a prophet from the Old Testament.

He was a highly skilled carpenter who loved plants, Tennessee, motorcycles, an English bulldog, his grandchildren, and me. Not necessarily in that order. A childhood filled with hard work, driving uncles to moonshine suppliers, and rescuing women.

Sometimes he would just appear as if by magic to "see if everything was ok" at my place. I knew he was always just a phone call away.

There is timing to relationships and as much as I loved having him in my life, it was not our time. I wrote this poem shortly after I moved and he had called to make sure I was ok, 800 miles away.

LL Walker

The Reward of Patience

I saw a dove flying high above the ocean. Seeking a place to land. When it landed it called to its mate, but there was no answer.

Repeatedly the dove called and waited, but no sound could be heard from her mate. Several days passed and still no response to her consistent call.

The dove knew that God had created her and loved her.

One day, several weeks later, the dove was sitting on a large rock by the water, watching the waves slowly ebb onto the shore. A cooing sound, ever so faintly, could be heard between the cresting of each wave.

The sound of her mate growing louder as the white foam of the waves washed to shore. He had been searching for her, but was beyond her call and did not hear her.

The patience of the doves to hold daily vigilance and have faith in their beloved one's safe return ultimately united the two.

 Patience and unwavering faith that God provides for his creations, most assuredly the mate designed specifically for us. All we must do is follow the faith of the doves, patiently waiting God's gift.

Author's Note:

Do you know those moments when you aren't sure if something really happened or you just dreamed it happened?

One cool spring Phoenix night, I had gone to bed early after working on several projects. I don't know how long I had been asleep, when an overwhelming urge to write descended on me. At that moment I thought I was dreaming.

I got up, went to the living room where I had left my laptop... didn't turn on any lights, sat down, wrote this poem, and went back to bed.

In the morning, I remembered my dream. As I do every morning, I make coffee, take my vitamins, and opened my laptop to read my email. There it was in perfect format, perfect spelling, and no editing required— the poem, "The Reward of Patience."

Somewhere between my conscious and unconscious mind was the gift of this poem from those who love me on the other side of the veil. A gift I am passing along to you.

LL Walker

Kylemore Abbey Gothic Church: A Love Story

A love to be forever remembered—man for woman. A small church built to her "loving memory" to serve throughout time as a place for strangers from faraway places to come and experience the holiness of the church and the memory of her.

The soft voices of harmonious song with the pure intent to bring souls closer to the maker serve as the background of a man's love.

For God so loved the world—and man so loved his chosen partner and mate. A moment in time captured for all who visit... forever ensuring the knowledge of the power love bestows on all.

Today I was admitted into a love story between Mitchell Henry and his beloved Margaret. While on their honeymoon, she admired this amazing 15,000-acre place of beauty and refuge...so he bought it for her.

When she died unexpectedly, he built the chapel...."the Gothic church" to always remember her and the love he had for her. What a wonderful way to pass an afternoon listening to the soft angelic music in the chapel on a brisk fall Irish day.

What must it be like?

What must this be like? To create in the heart and soul of a man – a yearning of all the senses and aspects of his being to want to always be close to you both on this side of the veil and the other.

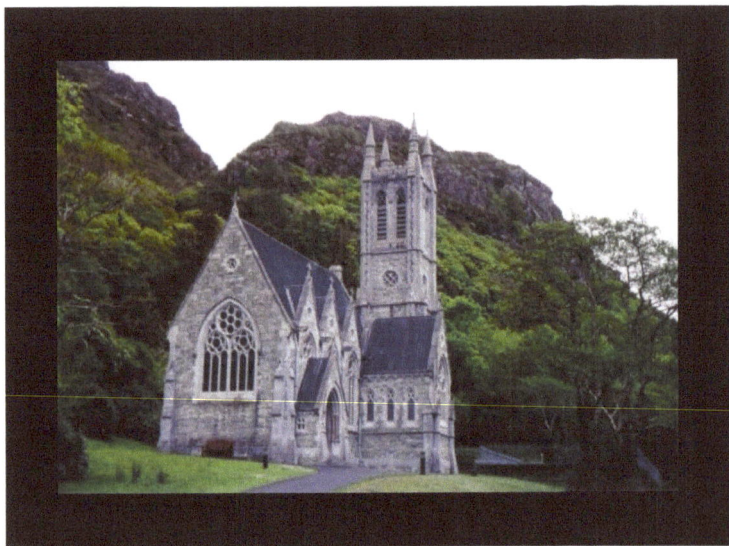

Oh to be worthy as a woman for the love of a man with such strength of character and ability to love. To be linked invisibly and for him to create–to build such a church for prayer–for the unification for love...

What must this be like?

The wonder created by this divine path of two creations–finding one another and generating a light so pure that others visit the site that documents the existence of their love decades later as a witness to these moments...

What must this be like?

.....Often we as women do not stop to ponder what do we do or how we are which would cause a man to love us as Mitchell Henry loved Margaret, as Darcy loved Elizabeth, or even as Romeo loved Juliet.

Are we worthy to be loved this deeply, completely, and passionately?? Should this first be our goal???

Author's Note:

Media interviews, hours by the shore reading and writing, nights filled with Irish music, a time of personal success and growth...I was in Ireland to help launch a book authored by Irish and Irish descendant professionals.

I love going to Ireland to walk in the history and feel the essence. A lovely country cottage in Conamara was my home for this month long visit.

Exploring the back roads by car, slowing for the sheep, the road curves. There before me was a scene from a Jane Austin move—the view of the prospect Elizabeth sees as she gazes at Darcy's estate—looking through a time window into the 1800s. I expected to see Darcy and Elizabeth strolling along the lake path. They weren't there, but an equally real life love story was.

As I walked along the path from the Downton Abby-like house, I found the ultimate love declaration; a chapel dedicated to the woman Mitchell Henry loved. A private serene spiritual place to sit among all those who had come before, I returned to this chapel of love many times during my time in Conamara.

Often in quiet meditative times, I mentally revisit the chapel. I didn't know the Henrys, but I am so very grateful Mitchell built this monument to remember Margaret, the love of his life.

LL Walker

Renewal

The clear evening sky twinkles with constellations from places we admire from afar. This is our silent time together at the end of each day. A glass of wine, curled up together under a warm clear summer evening in the mountains.

A perfect fit, your arm engulfs me as I snuggle up alongside you...my legs draped over yours. My head comfortably resting on your chest listening to your heart beat. Classical music quietly accompanies the night sounds.

We are physically and spiritually entwined as our auras blend together in perfect harmony and peace. No matter where we are, this time of day is always special and perfect.

As we transition to our bed, quietly chatting about the day or plans for tomorrow, serenity joins us. You turn out the light with one hand and reach for me with the other.

We sleep as one. Intertwined limbs, hand in hand, arms engulfing one another, moving in sync throughout the night. Sometimes you wake and I feel you lightly kiss me, as you change positions. Our lives are full. Our schedules hectic.... but in the still of the night, we find our refuge in one another, renewing our souls through our connectedness.

Morning arrives with ease, as I slide my hand across your chest to nudge you into consciousness. You smile; roll over to pull me even closer to you. Creatively exploring one another each morning, finding those special places of intensity, and heat launches our day bathed in love and often laughter welcoming the dawn. And so it is.

Author's Note:

Touching the person you choose for a moment in time to share your life has an internal intimacy difficult to explain to others. Calming, restful, contentment as the day slows seems incomplete without the touch. The ultimate in fully trusting in the love shared.

I once knew a power couple that seemed to have the world on a string. They built their lives and careers jointly balancing one another in perfect harmony. You could feel their intensity just being at dinner or in a meeting with them.

Sitting in an airport one day, I saw a couple who reminded me of what this couple could have looked like as the years would have passed. Although the couple I knew did not have the longevity together I was witnessing, I couldn't help but remember the time when the days and nights overflowed with the intensity of their touch.

LL Walker

Selfish Love...

Loving you is the most selfish thing I do.

In loving you, I feel peace and contentment

In loving you, I am excited by each new dawn

Loving you generates a joyous anticipation

It expands my heart, generating more love to give to all

For it is in loving you, I love myself and feel my Christ-ness

My vibrations increase, my energy enlarges, and I step lighter.

You see, Lord, loving you is the most selfish thing I do.

Author's Note:

Jesus loves me was one of the first songs I learned in Sunday school. Growing up, my grandmother would always talk to me about Gods love for me. My life has been a relentless pursuit of understanding love.

Trees are amazing companions. "The Giving Tree" is still one of my favorite books. It tells the story of a beautiful tree that loves a little boy unconditionally.

I have a favorite tree in a park not far from my home. In the summer I take a pillow, a book, and a picnic lunch and sit under the canopy of this beautiful oak tree.

It is all in the eyes

It's all in the eyes... in the depth of what one sees deep into the soul of an individual. It's the internal flutter, which accelerates your breathing when you first exchange glances; A hint of embarrassment at looking up and realizing that the person peering into your eyes is truly seeing you... all of you, into the center of your being.

It is not through the words spoken or the first touch that creates this accelerated heart beat or causes you to quickly look down trying to recover your composure.

He has captivated you, as was the original intent of the creator when Eve emerged from Adam's side and he first looked into her eyes.

There is certainly wonder and a joyful warmth when he places his hand in the small of your back to lead you protectively into a room, when he first takes your hand, strokes your hair, or when you feel the warmth of his breath so close to your ear, you begin to breathe in the same rhythm he does.

These are all responses engaging your physical receptivity to his gaze...the way he makes you feel when he simply looks at you.

It's in the eyes where he first makes his claim on you without hesitation even though he is uncertain of what your response will be.... This unrehearsed natural exchange seeing into the essence of someone you know... you know.

It is the eyes as he watches you; in the way he turns his head slightly to one side as if to see you more intently, closer, deeper.

It is in the eyes that you can see the love.... feel the intensity of his being as he walks toward you.

It is in the eyes as he pulls you closer. It is in the eyes as you move and he twinkles with excitement.

Later as the journey together evolves, it is the eyes, which reveal to you the security of his love, the safety of his protection, the longing of his soul.

It's in the eyes you find the missing piece planned for you to complete the circle of love in this lifetime. It's all in the eyes.

Author's Note:

This is one of my favorite poems. Each time I read it, I feel a swirling energy surround me creating warmth and joy. I love BBC period romance movies. The writers of the late 1700's and 1800's set off the romance fireworks with a subtle intensity that lasts page after page.

When BBC produced Elizabeth Gaskell's novel, "North and South" I settled in one chilly spring day to enjoy the journey through the English cotton industry romance she laid out so precisely in her work.

At the end of the movie, John Thornton looks into the face of Margaret Hale with an intensity that brings all those eye-to-eye moments you have experienced in your lifetime together in an overwhelming rush.

As the credits rolled, I collected my thoughts and wrote this collection of those visual exchanges I had experienced.

One at a time, they are lovely, but together they were enthralling. Reading this collection again and again, I realized, how I would know when the right love comes into my life...."it will all be in the eyes".

LL Walker

Did you know this

was love?

When you ask me to share your life, did you know the trials would strengthen our love?

When you didn't mention you filled the car up with gas because I pulled into the garage on empty...did you know this was the silence of love?

After a long tedious day at work, when what I really wanted was a long bubble bath and a glass of wine, but instead, I stopped to pick up your dry cleaning and your favorite desert.... did you know this was an act of love?

As we read through the Sunday paper looking for an afternoon excursion and you suggest we go to the art show instead of the baseball game.... did you know this was the selflessness of love?

When we look at one another in our seventies, we will see each other as we did in our twenties.... did you know this is the steadfastness of love?

Today, as I read to you your favorite sportswriter, and you forgot my name.... did you know this is part of the journey of love?

One day, when we join our friends and family on the other side...walking through the tunnel together into the light...did you know that this is the eternalness of love?

Author's Ending Note:

Love is a part of the human experience, mine, yours, the person seated next to you on the bus or subway; all those waiting in line with you at the store or seated close to you in a restaurant. Everyone has a story about love. Until next time.... don't let a moment pass without saying, "I love you" to those special people in your life.

LL Walker

About the Author

LL Walker probes the emotions, memories, and possibilities of the human experience. Her writing style pulls you into the experience with raw emotional authenticity. Her educational background in psychology creates unique windows into her characters, their motivations, and experiences.

Leah Lee Walker grew up in a small town in the Midwest. Her grandmothers provided a loving refuge filled with music, reading, colorful characters, and love.

Her first work for 2015, "Works of the Heart" is a collection of poems and passages documenting key life experiences. Be sure to check out her new Sunrise Ranch Saga where technology, tradition, laughter, and love intersect in powerful personal stories of the unexpected surprises life brings to the members of three Fifth Generation Irish ranching families.

WALKER PUBLICATIONS®

Walker Publications specializes in unique writers with innovative approaches to topics. Novice and experienced authors find the Walker process simple with a responsive staff to assist in the journey of publishing.

Poised at the leading edge of the "*New Way to Conduct Business*", Walker writers blend mind, body, and spirit in the essence of their writing to deliver holistic relevant works for individuals, groups, and organizations.

Making a difference in the lives of many through the dedication of a few focused on ...Putting thoughts into action.

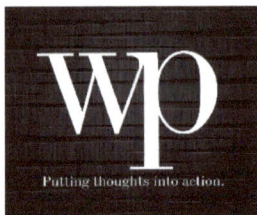

Walker Publications
…..Putting thoughts into action
E: walkerpublications3@gmail. com
W: www.walkerpublications.co
Twitter: @walker_pubs
Facebook: Walker Publications

www.ingramcontent.com/pod-product-compliance
Lightning Source LLC
Chambersburg PA
CBHW051234090426
42740CB00001B/11